CLARK COUNTY

D1405613

CLARK COUNTY

LAS VEGAS-CLARK COUNTY
LIBRARY DISTRICT
833 LAS VEGAS BLVD. N.
LAS VEGAS, NEVADA 89101

Science Matters! | Volume 24

How we see things

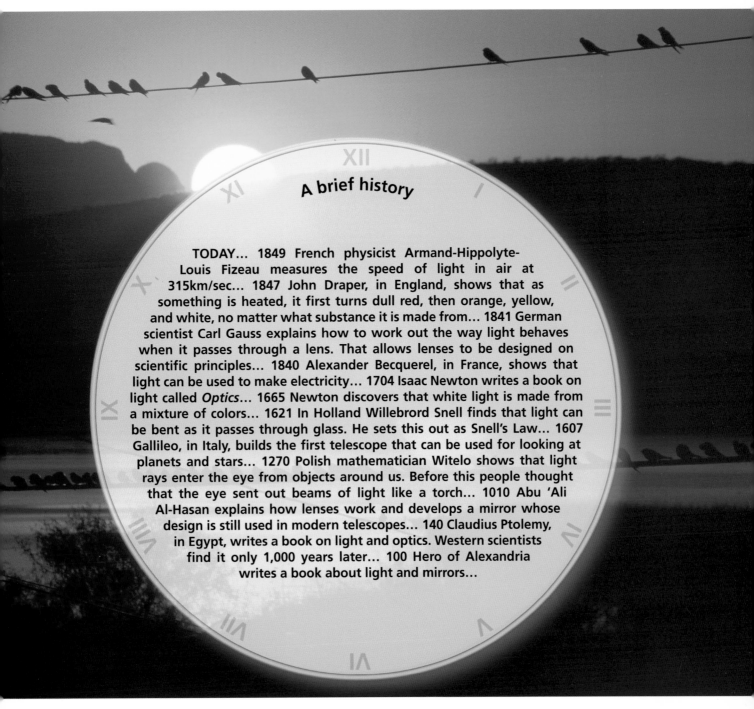

A brief history

TODAY... 1849 French physicist Armand-Hippolyte-Louis Fizeau measures the speed of light in air at 315km/sec... 1847 John Draper, in England, shows that as something is heated, it first turns dull red, then orange, yellow, and white, no matter what substance it is made from... 1841 German scientist Carl Gauss explains how to work out the way light behaves when it passes through a lens. That allows lenses to be designed on scientific principles... 1840 Alexander Becquerel, in France, shows that light can be used to make electricity... 1704 Isaac Newton writes a book on light called *Optics*... 1665 Newton discovers that white light is made from a mixture of colors... 1621 In Holland Willebrord Snell finds that light can be bent as it passes through glass. He sets this out as Snell's Law... 1607 Gallileo, in Italy, builds the first telescope that can be used for looking at planets and stars... 1270 Polish mathematician Witelo shows that light rays enter the eye from objects around us. Before this people thought that the eye sent out beams of light like a torch... 1010 Abu 'Ali Al-Hasan explains how lenses work and develops a mirror whose design is still used in modern telescopes... 140 Claudius Ptolemy, in Egypt, writes a book on light and optics. Western scientists find it only 1,000 years later... 100 Hero of Alexandria writes a book about light and mirrors...

Dr. Brian Knapp

Word list

These are some science words that you should look out for as you go through the book. They are shown using CAPITAL letters.

BEAM
A broad band or shaft of light such as that produced by a flashlight. Sunbeams are beams of sunlight.

CELL
The small building blocks that make up all living things. Cells are specialized to help the body in various ways. Rods and cones are cells in the eye that are sensitive to light and color.

CONCAVE MIRROR
A curved mirror in which the middle is further away from you than the edge. The inside of a dish-shaped mirror is concave.

CONVEX MIRROR
A curved mirror in which the middle is closer to you than the edge. A bulging mirror is convex.

ECLIPSE
The shadow made when the Moon comes between the Sun and the Earth. It is called an eclipse of the Sun. At this time the Moon is seen in silhouette as it casts a shadow over part of the Earth.

FIELD OF VIEW
The angle you can see. If the angle is narrow, you have a narrow field of view.

FOCUS
(a) To see things clearly.
(b) The point at which rays of light meet.

GLARE
Light that is so bright it makes you squint. Glare is often caused by light reflecting from a mirrorlike surface, such as water or cars.

LASER
A machine able to produce a very concentrated beam of light.

LENS
A curved piece of transparent material, such as glass, that makes light rays bend.

LIGHT-YEAR
The distance light travels in a year (nearly 10 trillion km).

OPAQUE
Something that light cannot get through. Opposite of transparent.

PINHOLE
A small hole through which light is shone. A pinhole can be used to make a sharp image.

RAY
A single line or narrow band of light. Light rays are much narrower than beams of light. Their main use in science is in tracing the path of light.

REFLECT
To bounce from a surface. Light reflects in much the same way as sound.

SHADOW
A dark or partly dark shape that is cast by an object when it blocks out rays of light.

SILHOUETTE
The black outline of an object when seen from its shadow.

SOURCE OF LIGHT
Something that gives out light. The Sun and other stars are the largest sources of light. Streetlights, fires, oil and gas lamps, and flashlights are other examples of sources of light.

SPECTRUM
The name given to all of the colors of visible light.

TRANSPARENT
Something that light will pass through easily. Opposite of opaque.

Contents

Light rays

Light travels in straight lines. We call a narrow BEAM of light a light ray.

Have you ever wondered how we see anything at all? Our eyes are not like flashlights, sending out light so that we can see. It's the other way around. Our eyes receive light. If no light entered our eyes, the world would seem black.

▼ **(Picture 1) Here you can see that light travels in straight lines. Sunlight is traveling through a misty forest, which picks out the beams of light.**

Sources of light

Anything that sends out light is called a **SOURCE OF LIGHT**. The Sun is the brightest natural source of light we have. Other natural sources include lightning, moonlight, and the light given by stars.

We produce light for ourselves from many other sources. Lamps are our most common source of light, but we sometimes use fires, fireworks, oil lights, gas lights, **LASERS**, and others.

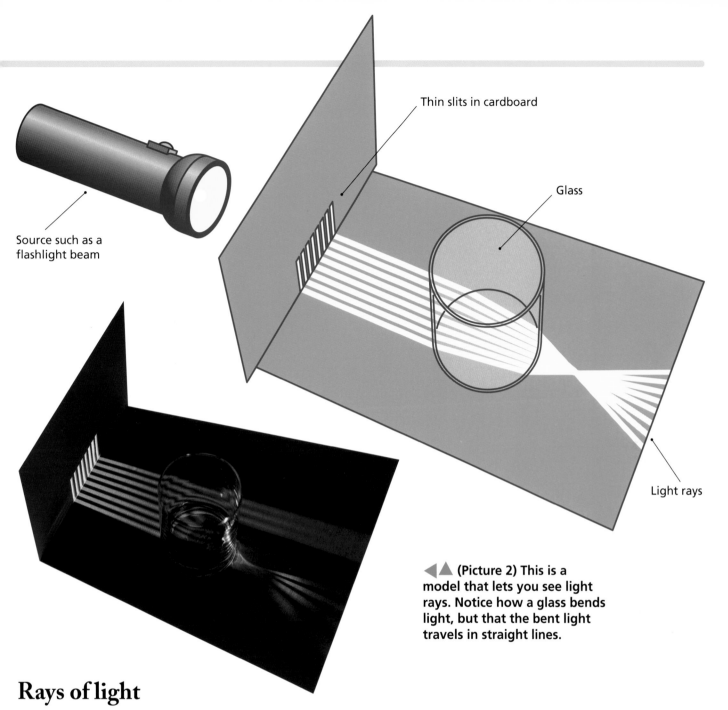

Source such as a
flashlight beam

Thin slits in cardboard

Glass

Light rays

◀▲ (Picture 2) This is a
model that lets you see light
rays. Notice how a glass bends
light, but that the bent light
travels in straight lines.

Rays of light

Light always travels outward in straight
lines. Light doesn't curve. You can see
this in nature when, for example, the Sun
shines through a misty forest (Picture 1).
But you can also show that light travels
in straight lines by setting up a model like
that shown in Picture 2.

In a darkened room, when light shines
through a piece of cardboard with thin
slits cut into it, you can see narrow shafts,
or **RAYS** of light.

Put a glass, or some other object that
lets light through, in the path of the rays.
You will now see that the light rays bend;
but, even when they are bent, the light
still travels in straight lines.

Summary
- **Light is produced by natural sources, like the Sun, or artificial ones such as lamps.**
- **Light always travels in straight lines.**
- **The path of a narrow beam of light is called a light ray.**

Shadows and silhouettes

We see things because rays of light reach our eyes. If no light reaches our eyes, we see nothing and call it darkness.

If you look around you, you will find that most objects are lighted well enough for us to see them. But often an object blocks out the light. There are two words we use when an object blocks out some or all of the light—SHADOW and SILHOUETTE.

Shadows

Things that block the path of light completely are called OPAQUE objects.

Because light travels in straight lines, it cannot curl around the sides of opaque objects that are in the way. The region behind the opaque object is then in darkness. The darkness is the same shape as the object that blocks out the light. It is the shadow (Picture 1).

Sharp and fuzzy shadows

Shadows are only sharp when there is just one small source of light. If the source of light is large, the shadow will have fuzzy edges, and it will not be completely dark.

Shadow sizes

Shadows are not the same size as the object that makes them. Picture 1 shows you why. The size of the shadow depends on the distance between the source of light, the object making the shadow, and the surface on which the shadow is made.

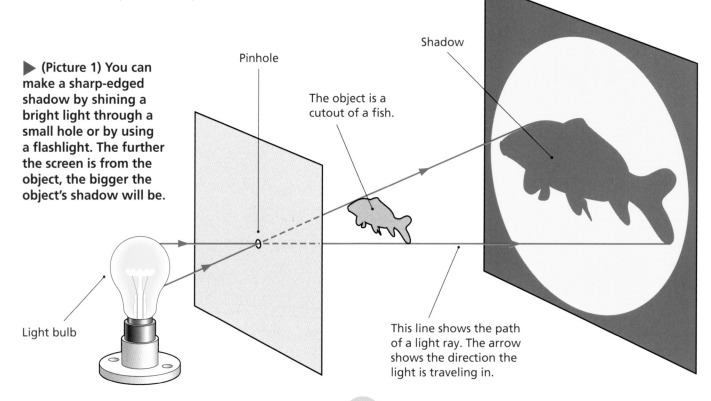

▶ (Picture 1) You can make a sharp-edged shadow by shining a bright light through a small hole or by using a flashlight. The further the screen is from the object, the bigger the object's shadow will be.

Pinhole

Shadow

The object is a cutout of a fish.

Light bulb

This line shows the path of a light ray. The arrow shows the direction the light is traveling in.

To help you see why this is so, the path of light is drawn as two straight lines coming from the light bulb. Each ray of light passes through the small hole (called a **PINHOLE**) and then grazes the sides of the object.

Because light travels in straight lines, the further the screen is behind the object, the bigger the shadow will be. In Pictures 2 and 3 the object and screen have each been moved to show you what effect this has.

Silhouette

So far, we have looked at the shadow cast by an object. But if you were standing in the shadow of an object, you would see the object as black, with a bright light around it. That is called a silhouette (Picture 4). During an **ECLIPSE** of the Sun,

▲ **(Picture 4) When you look at a bright light and see the outline of an object, the object appears black. That is called a silhouette.**

for example, the Moon's shadow is cast on the Earth, but we see the Moon in silhouette against the sunlit sky.

Summary
- **When light is blocked, it produces shadows and silhouettes.**
- **The size of a shadow changes depending on the distance between the source of light, the object, and the surface the shadow falls on.**
- **To get sharp shadows, there must be a single, small source of light.**

▼ **(Picture 2) Here the fish cutout has been moved closer to the source of light, and so the shadow is bigger.**

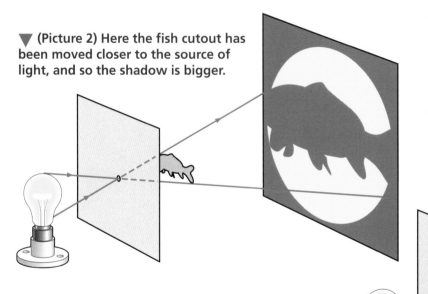

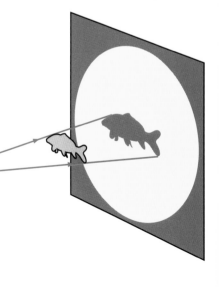

▶ **(Picture 3) Here the screen has been moved closer to the fish cutout, and so the shadow is smaller.**

How flat mirrors work

A flat mirror is something with a shiny surface that bounces all light in the same direction.

A mirror has a very flat, shiny surface that is very good at bouncing light. Most mirrors are made of glass that has a silvery coating on the back.

When you face a flat mirror, you can see yourself reflected very clearly (Picture 1). You also appear to be the same distance

► (Picture 1) If you look at yourself in a mirror, some of the light bouncing off you goes toward the mirror and is bounced back to your eye.

behind the mirror as you are in front of it. But everything you see is back to front.

Quite often we use mirrors for looking at ourselves, but they can also be used for seeing things when our view is blocked. A periscope is an example of this (Picture 2).

◄ (Picture 2) You can use two mirrors to make a periscope. People use periscopes to see over the heads of others in crowds, where it is impossible to get a direct view.

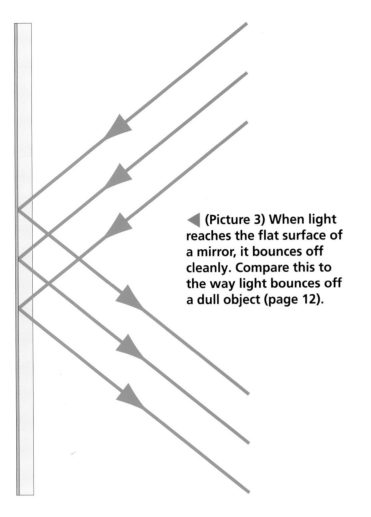

(Picture 3) When light reaches the flat surface of a mirror, it bounces off cleanly. Compare this to the way light bounces off a dull object (page 12).

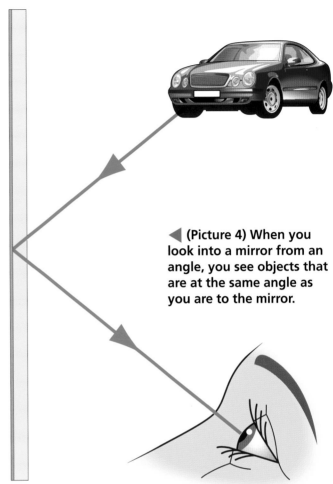

(Picture 4) When you look into a mirror from an angle, you see objects that are at the same angle as you are to the mirror.

How mirrors work

Light bounces off, or **REFLECTS** from, almost everything, but most objects are dull, not shiny like a mirror. A mirror has such a shiny surface that when light falls on it, the light rebounds cleanly (Picture 3). This means that we see a bright, clear reflection.

Angled mirrors

When you look into a mirror at an angle, you do not see yourself, but objects that are to one side of you (Picture 4). That

is because the light is reflected from the mirror at the same angle as it arrives.

By turning a mirror at an angle or looking at a mirror from the side, we can see things that would be out of our normal view. The wing mirrors on a car are examples of the way we use angled mirrors.

Summary

- A mirror can be made of any shiny material.
- Light that reaches a mirror bounces off at the same angle as it arrived.
- You can use mirrors to look at yourself and at things to one side or behind you.

Curved mirrors

When light is bounced from curved mirrors, the image changes shape.

Look at a spoon. Both sides are bright and shiny, but curved (Picture 1). Both sides are curved mirrors. The outside is a mirror that bulges, while the inside is a dish-shaped mirror. We use the term **CONVEX MIRROR** for a bulging mirror and **CONCAVE MIRROR** for a dished mirror. (You can remember concave as dish-shaped if you think that con*cave* is like the inside of a *cave*.)

Curved mirrors give you some surprising views of the world.

Convex mirrors

Bulging, or convex, mirrors show you a small image. Look carefully, and you will see that the shape has also been changed, or distorted, and that you get a wide **FIELD OF VIEW** (Picture 2). As a result, what you see appears smaller than it really is.

Bulging mirrors are used for rear-view mirrors in cars and for security mirrors in stores.

▼ **(Picture 1) You can find curved (and flat) mirrors every time you eat. Your spoon and fork are curved mirrors. The fork is only curved in one direction, while the spoon is dish-shaped. The knife is a flat mirror. The spoon is shown here. Find out for yourself what the fork and knife do.**

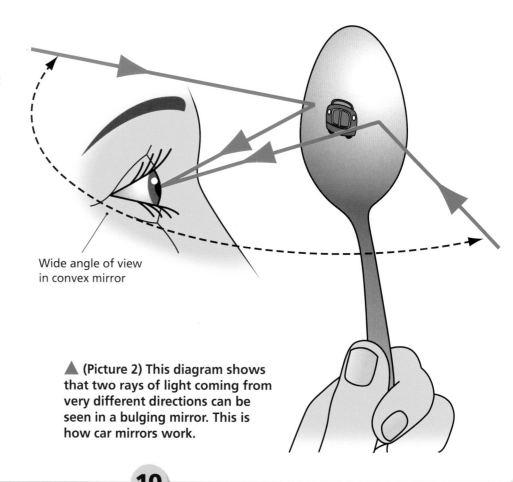

Wide angle of view in convex mirror

▲ **(Picture 2) This diagram shows that two rays of light coming from very different directions can be seen in a bulging mirror. This is how car mirrors work.**

Concave mirrors

Dish-shaped, or concave mirrors, like the inside of a spoon, give you a narrow field of view (Picture 3), so you need to look at them from close-up. These mirrors make an enlarged image (Picture 4).

Dish-shaped mirrors are used for shaving and makeup mirrors, but they are also used behind bulbs, as in a flashlight (Picture 5). Here their purpose is to send out light in a parallel beam.

Dish-shaped mirrors are also used to collect light. The world's biggest telescopes use dish-shaped mirrors to gather as much light as possible from distant stars. In this way dished mirrors allow us to see other worlds.

▲ (Picture 4) You can see the effect of a curved mirror more clearly with a large, flexible mirror like this one. When curved inward, the face appears wider.

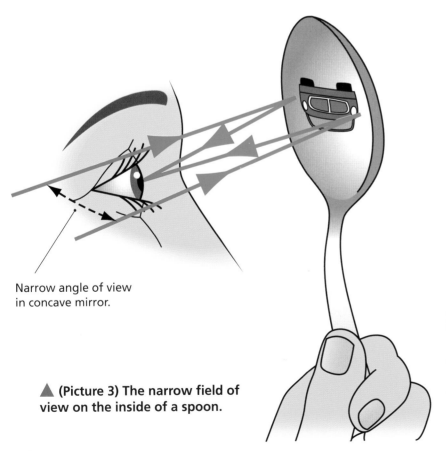

Narrow angle of view in concave mirror.

▲ (Picture 3) The narrow field of view on the inside of a spoon.

▲ (Picture 5) A concave mirror can be found behind the light in a flashlight.

Summary

- Bulging mirrors give a smaller (reduced) view of our surroundings.
- Dished mirrors give us an enlarged view.
- Curved mirrors always distort shapes.

Scattering and soaking up light

When light bounces from rough surfaces, some is soaked up, and the rest is scattered. Unless it is black, everything around us bounces some light from its surface.

If you look in a mirror, you will see yourself clearly and in full color. But other surfaces do not work like this. Here is the reason.

Scattering light

Only shiny surfaces, like spoons and glass, make mirrors. You cannot see a clear reflection in a surface that is not smooth.

When light reaches a rough surface, it is bounced off in all directions—it is scattered (Pictures 1, 2, and 3). Because light is scattered, we never see all the light from one object, and so we can never see a clear reflection.

Colored light

Most surfaces are not only rough, but they are also colored.

A mirror is *not* colored because it reflects nearly all of the light that hits its surface. However, most things soak up some of the light that reaches them. The more light they soak up, the darker they look. If they soak up all of the light, they are black (Picture 4).

White light is a mixture of all of the colors of the rainbow—we call it a SPECTRUM (Picture 5). Colored surfaces

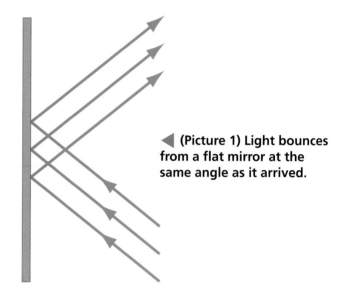

◀ **(Picture 1) Light bounces from a flat mirror at the same angle as it arrived.**

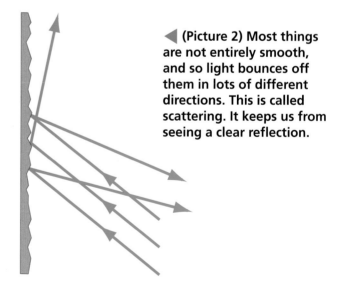

◀ **(Picture 2) Most things are not entirely smooth, and so light bounces off them in lots of different directions. This is called scattering. It keeps us from seeing a clear reflection.**

soak up only some parts of the white light. For example, a green object soaks up all light except green light, a blue object soaks up all of the colors in white light except blue, and so on.

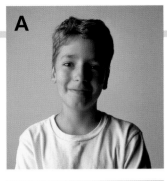

A

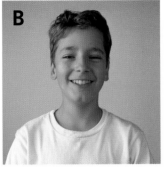

B

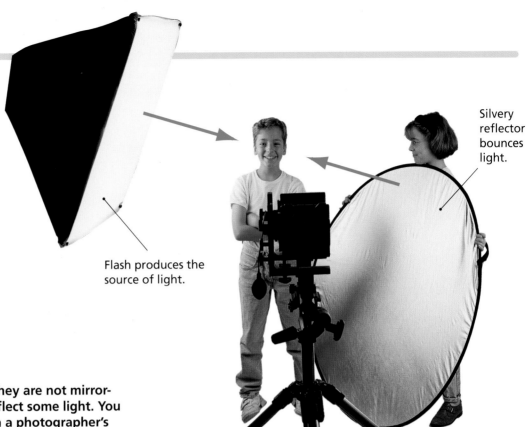

Silvery reflector bounces light.

Flash produces the source of light.

▲ **(Picture 3) Even though they are not mirror-shiny, nearly all materials reflect some light. You can see this property used in a photographer's studio. The main source of light is a powerful flash. If the photographer uses only this light, one side of the face will be in deep shadow (A). But if a silvery surface is also used, it reflects light back and reduces the darkness of the shadow (B).**

The fact that some of the light has been soaked up means that there is less light to reflect, which is why colored surfaces are darker than white ones.

White surfaces do not soak up more of one color than another. That is also why they appear bright.

▲ **(Picture 4) A white surface reflects a lot of the light that hits its surface, a black surface reflects very little light, and a gray surface is somewhere in between.**

Summary

• Most surfaces soak up some light.
• Lighter surfaces bounce back the most light.
• Scattered light makes shadows less dark.

▲ **(Picture 5) White light is a mixture of all the colors of the rainbow. When you pass light through a triangle of glass, all the colors are separated.**

We see like a camera

A simple pinhole camera will take pictures and also show you how the eye works.

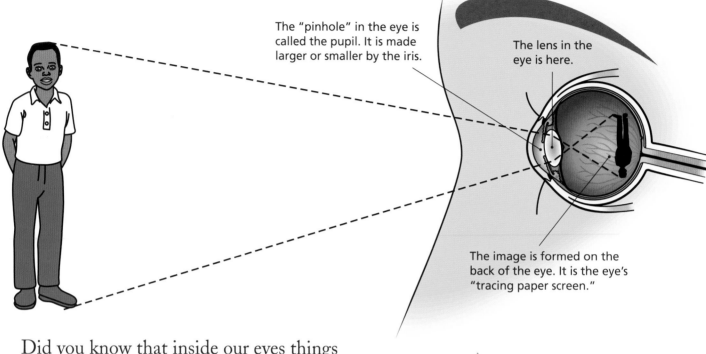

The "pinhole" in the eye is called the pupil. It is made larger or smaller by the iris.

The lens in the eye is here.

The image is formed on the back of the eye. It is the eye's "tracing paper screen."

Did you know that inside our eyes things appear upside down and back to front? It is only our brains that make sense of this and turn things the right way up (Picture 1).

Pinhole camera

To know why we see things upside down, we can make a very simple model of an eye. It is made of a tube with a small pinhole at one end and a sheet of tracing (or wax) paper over the other (Picture 2). It is called a pinhole camera. A pinhole camera is not just a model of the eye, it is also a model of how all cameras work. The first camera ever made was a pinhole camera.

Not much light passes through a pinhole, so the object you look at has to be very bright.

▲ (Picture 1) There is a lens inside the eye that turns images upside down and back to front.

▼ (Picture 2) A pinhole camera works on exactly the same principle as your eye, so you see things in just the same way as a pinhole camera.

▶ **(Picture 3)** Light travels only in straight lines, so light from the top of the lamp goes through the pinhole and hits the bottom of the screen. Similarly, light from the bottom of the lamp goes through the pinhole and hits the top of the screen. That is why the lamp appears upside down on the screen.

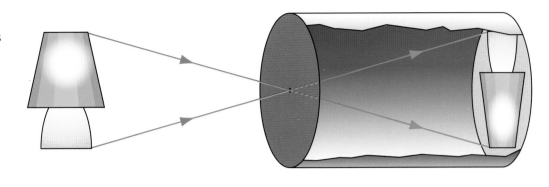

▶ **(Picture 4)** If you make the hole larger, light spreads out as it passes through the hole, and that makes a fuzzy image.

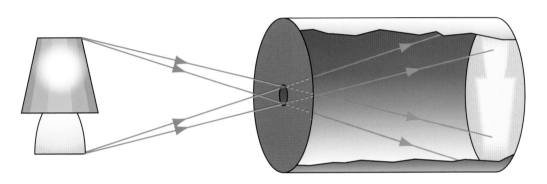

▶ **(Picture 5)** To get a bright image that is also in focus, you need to use a lens instead of a pinhole.

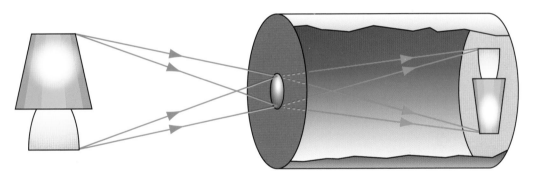

If you hold the pinhole camera to a lamp, for example, you will see an image of the lamp on the tracing paper screen. But the really strange thing is that the image of the lamp will be upside down and back to front (Picture 3).

Getting more light

Pinhole cameras make a really sharp image. But only when they use pin-sized holes. If you make the hole bigger to allow more light in, the image gets fuzzy (Picture 4). To get a bright image that is also sharp—called in **FOCUS**—you need a specially curved piece of glass or plastic called a **LENS** (Picture 5). That is why both eyes and cameras have lenses, not just pinholes.

Summary
- Our eyes are like pinhole cameras.
- Our eyes see upside down and back to front.
- Our eyes have a lens so that lots of light can be let in and still make a sharp image.

How the eye works

The eye contains a lens to focus light accurately and special cells that change light into signals which our brain can make sense of.

To sense the world around them, most animals have ways of detecting light. Many animals use eyes to help them see clear images.

Simple eyes

Some worms have very simple "eyes." They are just light-sensitive **CELLS** on parts of their skin.

Insect eyes are made of lots of small, fixed lenses. They are called compound eyes (Picture 1).

Human eyes

More complicated animals, such as humans, have eyes that can focus light and alter the amount of light reaching the eye. That is the job of the lens and the iris (Picture 2).

The back of a human eye (which is called the retina) is covered by millions of light-sensitive cells. Cells nearer the center of the retina are cone-shaped (cones), while those nearer the edge are rod-shaped (rods).

Light first travels through the front of the eye. This **TRANSPARENT** window is called the cornea. Because the cornea is curved, it behaves like a lens. It is where much of the light-gathering is done.

▲ (Picture 1) This is what an insect eye looks like. It consists of many simple, fixed lenses. Insect eyes do not move.

However, the cornea is not an adjustable lens. That is why the light then passes through the pupil of the eye. The iris is a thin, circular disk with a hole in the center called the pupil (Picture 3). It's something like a pinhole in the pinhole camera.

The light then passes through the lens, where focusing is fine-tuned. Finally, the light is focused on the retina.

The lens is made of elastic, transparent fibers. Over time, these fibers become less elastic, and it becomes harder for the eye to be fine-tuned into focus. That is when people need glasses.

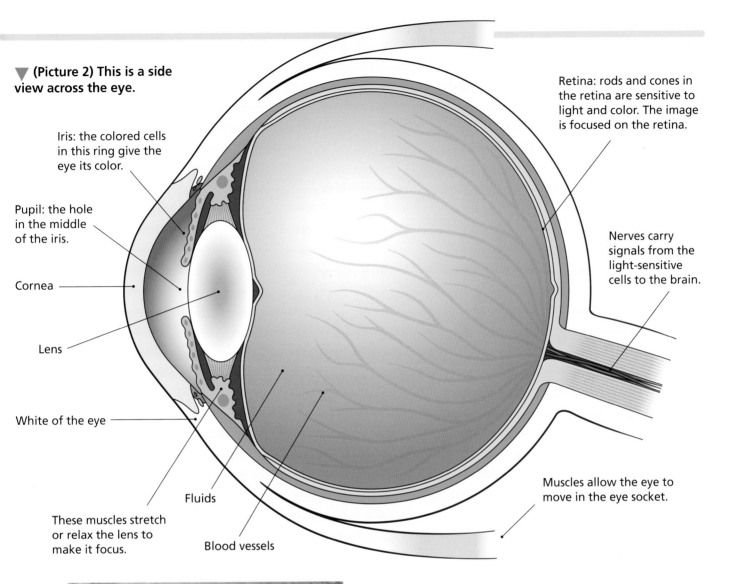

(Picture 2) This is a side view across the eye.

Iris: the colored cells in this ring give the eye its color.

Pupil: the hole in the middle of the iris.

Cornea

Lens

White of the eye

Fluids

These muscles stretch or relax the lens to make it focus.

Blood vessels

Retina: rods and cones in the retina are sensitive to light and color. The image is focused on the retina.

Nerves carry signals from the light-sensitive cells to the brain.

Muscles allow the eye to move in the eye socket.

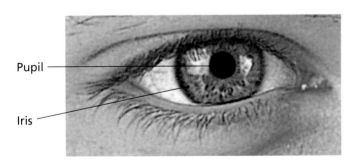

Pupil

Iris

▲ (Picture 3) The iris can open up the pupil to let in more light. It can also reduce the size of the pupil, but it cannot close the pupil completely.

The human eye is designed to see through air. That is why it is so difficult to see underwater. The tissues of the eye are made mostly of water, so the eye does not bend the light as much in water as it does in air. That is why you need a face mask to see clearly underwater.

Summary
- The eye is ball-shaped, with a front section that lets light in.
- The light is focused by the cornea and fine-tuned by the lens.
- The light is focused on the back of the eye, where special cells change light to electrical signals that are sent to the brain.

Glasses

Most people will need the help of eyeglasses during their lives. This is what glasses do.

Our eyes have natural lenses in them. These lenses can change shape, as we saw on page 16. That allows us to focus on things that are close at hand and far away (Picture 1).

Sometimes our eyes are not able to give us a very clear picture. That is because the natural lenses in our eyes cannot change to the shape we need. When that happens, we help the eye by adding an extra lens in front. These lenses include glasses and hand lenses (Picture 2).

There are two kinds of lenses, those that are slightly bulging (called convex lenses) and those that are slightly dished (called concave lenses).

How glasses are made

Lenses begin as a sheet of glass or plastic and are then shaped using fine sanding powder and specially shaped tools. Contact lenses are small lenses held on the surface of the eye.

Since plastic is less dense than glass, plastic glasses are not as heavy. Plastic scratches more easily than glass, but it is less brittle and less likely to shatter.

Sunglasses often contain no lenses at all and are simply sheets of glass or plastic coated with material that soaks up some of the light passing through them. Tinted coating can also be applied to lenses.

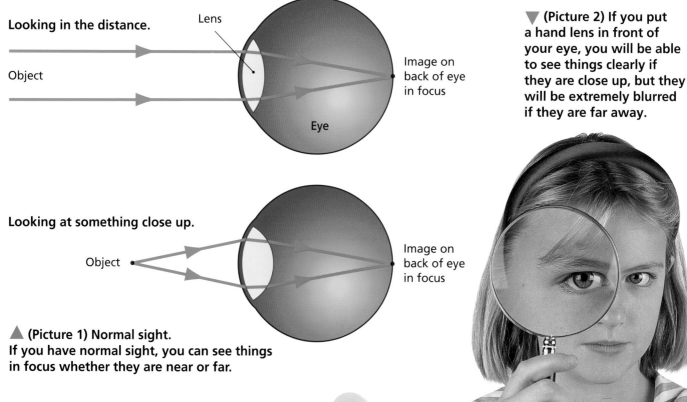

Looking in the distance.

Lens

Object

Image on back of eye in focus

Eye

Looking at something close up.

Object

Image on back of eye in focus

▲ **(Picture 1) Normal sight.**
If you have normal sight, you can see things in focus whether they are near or far.

▼ **(Picture 2) If you put a hand lens in front of your eye, you will be able to see things clearly if they are close up, but they will be extremely blurred if they are far away.**

How glasses work for short-sighted people

Some people can see near things clearly, but distant things look blurred (Picture 3). In this case the lens of the eye brings light into focus before it reaches the back of the eye. To correct this problem, a dished lens is used to change the direction of the light before it reaches the eye. This focuses light correctly on the back of the eye.

How glasses work for far-sighted people

Many people can see distant things clearly, but closeup things look blurred (Picture 4). This is the more usual eye problem. In this case the lens of the eye brings light to a focus behind the back of the eye. To correct this problem, a slightly bulging lens is needed to bring objects to a focus exactly at the back of the eye.

Summary

- Glasses are a way to help improve sight.
- Slightly dished lenses help correct short-sightedness.
- Slightly bulging lenses help correct far-sightedness.

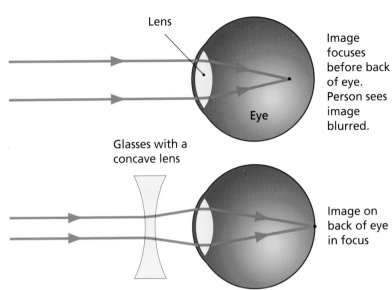

▲ (Picture 3) Short-sightedness.
The upper diagram shows a side view of the eye of someone with short-sightedness and without glasses. Light from objects a long way away focuses before it reaches the back of the eye.

The bottom diagram shows how a concave lens keeps the light from focusing too soon, so that it focuses exactly on the back of the eye.

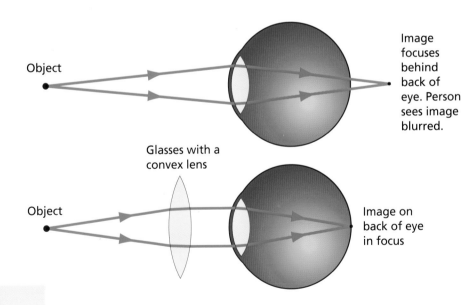

▲ (Picture 4) Far-sightedness.
The upper diagram shows a side view of the eye of someone with far-sightedness and without glasses.

The bottom diagram shows how a bulging (convex) lens focuses the light sooner, so that it focuses exactly on the back of the eye.

Why distant things look dim and small

Light spreads out from an object. The further from the object you are, the less of the light you receive, and the dimmer it seems.

The Sun looks very bright—in fact, it is so bright that we cannot safely look at it directly. But if we were to visit Mercury, the planet nearest the Sun, or Pluto, the planet furthest from the Sun, would the Sun look the same? To find out, we can use a bulb as a model Sun.

When light spreads out

A light bulb, like the Sun, is a source of light (Picture 1). The bulb gives out a certain amount of light, which spreads out in all directions. If we are close to the bulb, for example, a meter away, a large proportion of the light enters our eyes (this is shown by the shape at **A** in Picture 1). But as we move further away, a smaller and smaller proportion of the light reaches us. The rest goes to light the room. When we are twice as far from the bulb, we only receive a quarter as much light, so the lamp appears a quarter as bright (**B**). When we are 3 metres away from the bulb, only a ninth as much light enters our eyes as when we were 1 metre away (**C**).

▼ **(Picture 1) As light spreads out, it covers a bigger and bigger area. The same light that covers the square A at 1m, has to spread out to cover four times the area by the time it reaches B and nine times the area when it reaches C. That is why lights look dimmer as we move away from them.**

Light bulb

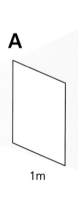

A

1m

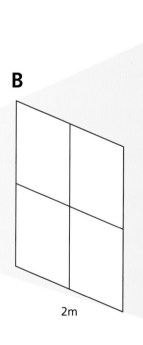

B

2m

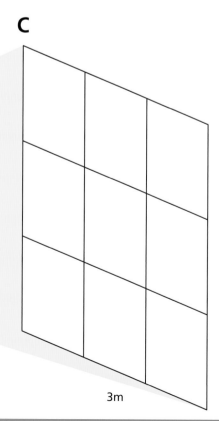

C

3m

(Picture 2) If we were to visit the planet Mercury, which is two-thirds closer to the Sun than the Earth is, the Sun would appear to be a huge, bright disk. Pluto is forty times farther away from the Sun than the Earth is, and so from Pluto the Sun would appear hardly brighter than any other star.

The same thing is true of the stars in the night sky. Many stars are thousands of times bigger and brighter than our Sun; but because they are far away, we receive such a tiny part of their light that they appear small and dim. The picture below shows an exploding star billions of LIGHT-YEARS away. It was taken by the Hubble space telescope.

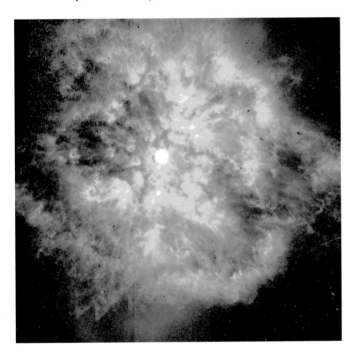

As you can see, the brightness of light appears to fall very sharply indeed the further we move away from it. The light, of course, stays the same brightness. It is just that less of it reaches our eyes (Picture 2).

Why distant things look small

Hold a marble close to your eye (Picture 3). It will look quite large. Now hold it at arm's length, and it will look much smaller.

The marble is the same size; it just appears to have changed size.

How big something appears depends on how much of our view it uses up. It is the same reasoning that explains why distant things look dim. When something is close, it fills up much of the area our eyes can see, and so it appears large and in a lot of detail. When something is further away, it takes up only a small amount of the area that we can see, and so it seems small.

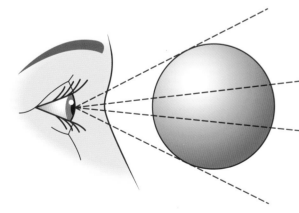

▲ (Picture 3) As objects get further away, they appear smaller because they take up less of our field of view.

Summary

- Bright objects appear dim when they are far off because only a tiny part of their light reaches our eyes.
- Objects appear small when they take up only a small part of our view.

Cutting out glare

Ordinary sunglasses cut down the light, but polaroid sunglasses also cut out glare.

▲ (Picture 1) Glare is a particular problem with mirrorlike surfaces such as water, windows, or the metalwork of cars.

Ordinary sunglasses are made of material that partly blocks out the light. That is done by coating the surface of the glasses with a thin film of dark-colored material or adding dark coloring to the plastic as it is made. As a result, everything is made darker.

Polarizing glasses

Even when you have sunglasses on, a bright light reflecting from metal, glass, or water can cause an unpleasant GLARE (Pictures 1 and 2).

◀ (Picture 2) Glare is a common experience; and to cope with it, people wear sunglasses.

▲▼ (Picture 3) By cutting out reflection, polarizing filters allow you to see through the glare, for example, to see the stems of these lilies or perhaps fish gliding through the water.

That is because these surfaces behave like mirrors and send the light directly to your eye. All other surfaces are rough and scatter the light, so less of it reaches your eye. This contrast is what we mean by glare.

Polarizing sunglasses are made of a special material that cuts out some of the rays of reflected light, but lets others through unaltered. As a result, very bright, glaring, reflecting subjects produce less glare, while everything else is left undimmed.

Polarizing filters

Cameras can be equipped with special filters that cut out much of the glare. They are called polarizing filters.

To understand how they work, think of dropping a stone into a pond and watching the ripples spread out. This pattern of ripples (waves) is how light spreads out. The difference is that we cannot see light waves.

A polarizing filter is designed to cut out waves coming in the direction that causes glare. If you hold a filter to a glaring subject, such as a light being reflected from a pond, then turn the polarizing filter, you will see the glare reduce as the filter cuts out some of the waves (Picture 3).

Cut out light completely

If you hold one polarizing filter in front of another and turn one of them, a point will be reached when they have cut out nearly all of the light, and you see almost nothing.

Summary
- When we look at mirrorlike surfaces, light causes a glare.
- Sunglasses dim the glare but make everything else dark as well.
- Polarizing filters cut out unwanted reflections.

Index

Science Matters!

Grolier Educational

First published in the United States in 2003 by Grolier Educational, Sherman Turnpike, Danbury, CT 06816

Copyright © 2003
Atlantic Europe Publishing Company Ltd.

All rights reserved. No part of this publication may be reproduced, stored in a retrieval system, or transmitted in any form or by any means— electronic, mechanical, photocopying, recording, or otherwise—without prior permission of the publisher.

This product is manufactured from sustainable managed forests. For every tree cut down at least one more is planted.

Author
Brian Knapp, BSc, PhD

Educational Consultant
Peter Riley, BSc, C Biol, MI Biol, PGCE

Art Director
Duncan McCrae, BSc

Senior Designer
Adele Humphries, BA, PGCE

Editor
Lisa Magloff, BA

Illustrations
David Woodroffe

Designed and produced by
Earthscape Editions

Reproduced in Malaysia by
Global Color

Printed in Hong Kong by
Wing King Tong Company Ltd

Picture credits
All photographs are from the Earthscape Editions photolibrary.

Library of Congress Cataloging-in-Publication Data
Knapp, Dr. Brian J.
    Science Matters! / [Dr. Brian J. Knapp].
        p. cm.
    Includes index.
    Summary: Presents information on a wide variety of topics in basic biology, chemistry, and physics.
    Contents: v. 1. Food, teeth, and eating—v. 2. Helping plants grow well—v. 3. Properties of materials—v. 4. Rocks and soils—v. 5. Springs and magnets—v. 6. Light and shadows—v. 7. Moving and growing—v. 8. Habitats—v. 9. Keeping warm and cool—v. 10. Solids and liquids—v. 11. Friction—v. 12. Simple electricity—v. 13. Keeping healthy—v. 14. Life cycles—v. 15. Gases around us—v. 16. Changing from solids to liquids to gases—v. 17. Earth and beyond—v. 18. Changing sounds—v. 19. Adapting and surviving—v. 20. Microbes—v. 21. Dissolving—v. 22. Changing materials—v. 23. Forces in action—v. 24. How we see things—v. 25. Changing circuits.
    ISBN 0-7172-5834-3 (set)—ISBN 0-7172-5835-1 (v. 1)—ISBN 0-7172-5836-X (v. 2)—ISBN 0-7172-5837-8 (v. 3)—ISBN 0-7172-5838-6 (v. 4)—ISBN 0-7172-5839-4 (v. 5)—ISBN 0-7172-5840-8 (v. 6)—ISBN 0-7172-5841-6 (v. 7)—ISBN 0-7172-5842-4 (v. 8)—ISBN 0-7172-5843-2 (v. 9)—ISBN 0-7172-5844-0 (v. 10)—ISBN 0-7172-5845-9 (v. 11)—ISBN 0-7172-5846-7 (v. 12)—ISBN 0-7172-5847-5 (v. 13)—ISBN 0-7172-5848-3 (v. 14)—ISBN 0-7172-5849-1 (v. 15)—ISBN 0-7172-5850-5 (v. 16)—ISBN 0-7172-5851-3 (v. 17)—ISBN 0-7172-5852-1 (v. 18)—ISBN 0-7172-5853-X (v. 19)—ISBN 0-7172-5854-8 (v. 20)—ISBN 0-7172-5855-6 (v. 21)—ISBN 0-7172-5856-4 (v. 22)—ISBN 0-7172-5857-2 (v. 23)—ISBN 0-7172-5858-0 (v. 24)—ISBN 0-7172-5859-9 (v. 25)
    1. Science—Juvenile literature. [1. Science.] I. Title.

Q163.K48 2002
500—dc21

2002017302

3 1133 04848 7633